The
New Creation

Unfolding Grace

Vol 1

Apostle, Dr. Craig A. Comanche

ISBN:

DEDICATION

This book is dedicated to the Family of Believers in the Body of Christ and to my Lord and Savior Jesus Christ, the Son of the Living God and the Holy Spirit who is always with me accompanying me on this journey. Without these three, none of this would be possible. I thank You Father God for choosing me with this revelation of the New Creation. I pray that you find my diligence to see my assignment through pleasing before your eyes. Amen

TABLE OF CONTENTS

INTRODUCTION:
BECOMING WHAT GOD HAS ALREADY DECLARED

The message of the New Creature is not a new revelation—it is an eternal reality finally being unveiled in clarity and power. It is not simply a call to behave better, to become more religious, or to adopt a new set of rules. No, this is the divine unveiling of identity. A holy disruption of everything you thought you knew about yourself. In Christ, you are not being *improved*—you have been *reborn*.

For years, many believers have lived beneath their divine right—not because God withheld anything, but because our minds were never renewed to the truth of what He finished. We've shouted over blessings, danced over promises, and recited scriptures about victory—all while still living under the residue of a fallen mindset. But the old man is dead. Not wounded. Not weakened. **Dead.** And what stands in his place is **a new creature**, birthed from incorruptible seed, made alive with Christ, and seated in heavenly places.

The New Covenant didn't just give you access to God—it made you one with Him in spirit. You are now a partaker of His divine nature (2 Peter 1:4). You have been authorized to function on earth with heavenly backing. But how can you manifest what you've never been taught to believe about yourself?

This book is not a motivational push. It is a prophetic unveiling. A line-in-the-sand declaration that you will no longer be ignorant of your spiritual DNA. The truths within these pages will challenge your old belief systems, confront your carnal patterns, and awaken the new man within you. They are messages born in the presence of God—written through encounters, revelation, and a divine burden to see the body of Christ rise to her full identity.

You are not a better version of your old self. You are **a new creature**, one who never existed before. You have a new covenant written in the blood of Jesus. A new mind, renewed by the Word. A new assignment, revealed by the Spirit. And a new life—not someday, but now.

4

This journey isn't about trying to become something. It's about manifesting who you already are. Everything Jesus died to give you is not waiting on a future version of you—it's already yours. The question is, will you believe it?

This is your awakening. Welcome to the life of the New Creature.

CHAPTER 1:

MANIFESTING THE NEW CREATION

Scripture Foundation: 2 Corinthians 5:14–17; Colossians 3:10; Proverbs 22:9

"Therefore if any man be in Christ, he is a new creature: old things are passed away; behold, all things are become new."
—2 Corinthians 5:17

To be *in Christ* is not a poetic metaphor—it is a spiritual relocation. It is to be removed from one realm and placed into another. You are no longer merely a man trying to follow God; you have become a new being entirely—*born of God*, filled with His Spirit, and awakened to a reality beyond this natural world. The challenge isn't that you're not new—it's that you haven't fully believed or manifested what that newness means.

Manifestation begins with belief. Belief begins with revelation. And revelation only comes by the Spirit.

Too many believers still operate from a fallen identity while wearing the name of Jesus. They pray like orphans, worship like servants, and live like survivors—when God has called them sons. What would shift in your life if you truly believed that the old you—your sinful nature, your broken past, your fear, insecurity, and generational weight—*was nailed to the Cross* and buried with Christ?

Because it was.

When you were born again, you didn't receive a spiritual band-aid—you were re-created. You were made entirely new. But here's the truth most don't teach: **you cannot become the New Creature without receiving the New Life.** And that life is not earned; it is received.

Unfolding Grace Through Revelation

Paul said, *"I am what I am by the grace of God"* (1 Corinthians 15:10). Grace is not just unmerited favor—it is divine empowerment. It's heaven's enablement to walk in what God has spoken about you. But this grace must be received by **revelation**, not routine. If your mind remains in the old realm, you will sabotage the new life you've received.

That's why you can be saved and still stuck. You've heard the message, but your mind hasn't caught up with your spirit. The New Creature lives by *renewed knowledge* (Colossians 3:10), not by recycled experiences. The unfolding of grace is a process of revelation—seeing what God has already declared and aligning your thoughts, speech, and actions with it.

You don't need to be better—you need to *believe differently*.

Paul declared, *"I am what I am by the grace of God"* (1 Corinthians 15:10). Grace is more than a covering for sin—it is the divine enablement to become what God has already called you. But grace doesn't work in the shadows of tradition or routine. **Grace must be revealed before it can be walked in.** And when it is, it demands a response—not just of faith, but of boldness.

There is a kind of boldness that comes only from revelation. Not just boldness to speak—but boldness to live. **To walk away**

from what was familiar. To step into what has no natural blueprint. To become what no one in your bloodline has ever seen. This kind of boldness does not come from motivation. It comes from **hearing God speak to the new man you've become.**

The life you've been given is supernatural—and **you've never lived it before.** It's not just new to you—it's completely foreign to the carnal mind. You can't rely on your past to navigate it. You can't pull wisdom from your upbringing or lean on natural instincts. **God must guide you into the life He gave you.** The same Spirit who raised Christ from the dead is now your GPS, your Counselor, your Revealer. Without His guidance, you will default to old patterns while holding a new identity.

Revelation is your roadmap. Without it, you may have a new title (new creature) but keep walking in old territory. That's why the enemy isn't just after your behavior—he's after your revelation. Because once you *see* who you are, you'll start living like it. And once you start living like it, you become a threat to every kingdom of darkness.

God has not called you to survive this new life—He's called you to **master it**. And He doesn't expect you to figure it out on your own. The Holy Spirit will *guide you into all truth* (John 16:13). That's not just theological truth— it's personal truth. He will show you the dimensions of yourself that you didn't know existed. He will teach you how to talk, walk, lead, love, think, and build in a way that reflects heaven—not your history.

This is why revelation matters.

Because without it, you will shrink your divine identity to fit your human experience. But with it, you will rise—bold, confident, and fully persuaded—that who God says you are is who you really are.

See It. Speak It. Walk In It.

"Think the thoughts. Say the words. Receive the results."

That's what you wrote in the journal. And it's the rhythm of manifestation. As a new creature, you don't respond to circumstances the way you used to. Your thoughts are rooted in truth, your words carry spiritual authority, and your results reflect heaven's blueprint. But it all begins in your mind.

Let this truth settle: **You are no longer the person who went through that.** You are no longer the man who struggled, the woman who was abandoned, the person who failed. That version of you died. And if it died, it no longer has authority over your future.

The sooner you stop negotiating with your past, the sooner you will start creating with your new nature.

Living from Heaven's Viewpoint

The New Creature doesn't live from the ground up—he lives from the Spirit down. You are seated in heavenly places, even while you walk on earth. This dual reality gives you a kingdom perspective in natural circumstances. You no longer react to life as a victim—you respond to it as one who has *dominion*.

Proverbs 22:9 speaks of the "bountiful eye." In the Spirit, your eyes have changed. You no longer look at life through the lens of fear, lack, or self-doubt. You see with clarity, wisdom, and purpose. You perceive value where others see waste. You see kingship in those labeled as lost. And most importantly, you now see **yourself** as God sees you.

You Are a Living Revelation

Every time you believe in truth, you manifest Christ. The New Creature is not just someone who knows the Word—it is someone who **becomes** the Word in the earth. Your life becomes a living epistle, read by all men (2 Corinthians 3:2–3). Your presence becomes prophetic. Your speech becomes healing. Your decisions become kingdom strategies.

But none of this happens automatically. It happens by revelation, decision, and alignment.

You must decide to live from your new nature daily.

You must align your thoughts with your identity.

You must let go of what's dead so you can hold what's alive.

You must stop asking God to change you and start thanking Him that you've been changed.

You are not on your way to becoming—you already *are*. The moment you believed, heaven declared you new. Now it's time for Earth to agree.

Prayer for Manifesting the New Creation

Heavenly Father, I pray now that the eyes and the understanding of every reader be opened to receive and implement, in their spirit, the truth of their identity. Lord, I thank You that the revelation of our newness—that we have never been here before—is grasped deeply in the inner man.

I thank You, Lord, that this revelation produces a boldness to live out what You have called us to be: sons, not beggars. I thank You for the finished work of Christ, and I declare by faith that we are new creatures, filled with Your Spirit, alive in Your love, and seated with You in heavenly places.

We receive it. We walk in it. We manifest it.

In Jesus' name, Amen.

You are the New Creature. Manifest Him.

CHAPTER 2:

THE MINISTRY OF
RECONCILIATION

Scripture Foundation: 2 Corinthians 5:18–19; Philippians 2:5–11; Hebrews 8:10–12

"And all things are of God, who hath reconciled us to himself by Jesus Christ, and hath given to us the ministry of reconciliation."
—2 Corinthians 5:18

The ministry of reconciliation is not a job title—it's a divine operation. It is the unseen work of the Spirit to bring heaven and earth, God and man, spirit and soul, into one unified purpose. It is heaven's initiative, not man's effort. And it begins with the mind.

"Let this mind be in you, which was also in Christ Jesus."

This is not simply a call to humility—it's a call to divine alignment. In reconciliation, the mind of separation must be crucified. You cannot be reconciled and still see yourself as distant from God. The cross has settled the issue of access. **There is no more separation in the mind.** What kept man at a distance— sin, guilt, shame—was dealt with harshly on the Cross, once and for all. There's nothing left to pay.

This truth is not intellectual. It is spiritual. **It cannot be received by the natural mind.** It's a divine reality that must be born in your spirit and renewed in your thinking. Until that shift happens, you will live saved but still condemned, forgiven but still afraid, loved but still hiding. But reconciliation removes all fear and brings you boldly into the presence of the Father—not as a sinner begging for mercy, but as a son standing in love.

The Divine Exchange

Reconciliation is the divine exchange of separation for oneness. God was not content to relate to us from a distance. He came *in the flesh* to remove the barrier. He didn't just forgive us—He took it a step further: He **reconciled** us. That means He restored our relationship, unity, and shared identity. He made us sons again.

And this wasn't done lightly. The New Covenant was enacted with blood. **Sin was dealt with brutally—on purpose.** Jesus didn't die to excuse sin. He died to kill it. Not just some sin. **All sin**—past, present, and future— for all who believe. Heaven needed the issue of sin settled so reconciliation could be offered without condition. And it has been.

This is why there is **no record** of your faults in the heavenly realm. Your history has been erased. Your shame has been removed. Your record has been sealed—not hidden, **erased**—by the blood of the Lamb. Why? Because those things are not permitted there. And what's not permitted in heaven must no longer be permitted in your mind.

The Danger of a Weak Conscience

One of the greatest hindrances to a believer walking in the new life is a **weak conscience**. A conscience still carrying the memory of failure, still defining itself by the past, still wrestling with guilt. This weakens faith. It weakens identity. And ultimately, it weakens your ability to manifest sonship.

This is why the message of reconciliation must be preached—not just to the world, but to the Church. We need to stop reminding people how wrong they are and start revealing how loved they are. The power to change is in the revelation of **love**, not law. The law exposes sin, but love expels it. The law brings knowledge of guilt, but love brings knowledge of righteousness.

When a believer truly receives reconciliation, their conscience becomes clean. Their mind becomes renewed. Their spirit becomes bold. Why? Because the fear of being separated from God is gone. The fear of not being enough is gone. The voice of shame is silenced. And the voice of the Father becomes louder than the voice of failure.

What the World Needs Now

This is the ministry the world is waiting for—not another sermon on sin, but a revelation of **Sonship**.

The world is not starving for judgment—it's starving for reconciliation. They don't need to be beaten down with how wrong they are. They need to be lifted by the truth of how loved they are. God reconciled the world to Himself through Christ, **not imputing their trespasses unto them**, and committed to us the word of reconciliation (2 Corinthians 5:19). That's our message.

We are not ambassadors of wrath—we are **ambassadors of reconciliation**. We stand in the gap with a message that shatters guilt and restores dignity. We speak to dry bones and call them sons. We look at broken people and see kings. We declare, "Come home," not "Prove yourself." Because Jesus already did the proving—and we now do the calling.

He Calls Us Sons

Reconciliation is not complete until identity is restored. You are not just forgiven—you are named. And that name is **son**.

That's what makes reconciliation so powerful: God didn't just call you "not guilty." He called you **Mine**.

Heaven didn't open the gates just to let you in—it opened the house to seat you at the table. It welcomed you not as a visitor but as family. And now, we go to the world and do the same. We preach a gospel that **erases shame**, **restores purpose**, and **reveals sonship**.

This is the ministry we carry. This is the message that transforms.

This is reconciliation.

Prayer for Reconciliation and Identity

Father, I thank You for reconciling me to Yourself through Jesus Christ. Thank You that I am no longer separated from You but welcomed, embraced, and called Your own.

Renew my mind with the truth of reconciliation. Let guilt be silenced. Let shame fall away. Let every lie of unworthiness be destroyed in the light of Your love. I receive my place in the family of God. I receive my assignment as a minister of reconciliation.

Use me to heal the broken. Use me to speak truth in love. Use me to carry the fragrance of grace everywhere I go. Let others see You in me. Let the lost hear You calling through my voice.

I declare I am not condemned. I am accepted. I am not ashamed. I am bold. I am not striving. I am sent.

In Jesus' name, Amen.

CHAPTER 3:

THE MIND OF THE NEW MAN

Scripture Foundation: Romans 12:2; John 1:13; John 14:6; 1 Corinthians 2:16

"Be not conformed to this world: but be ye transformed by the renewing of your mind, that ye may prove what is that good, and acceptable, and perfect, will of God."
—Romans 12:2

The New Man is not just spiritually alive—he is **mentally transformed**. The mind of the New Man has undergone a death and a resurrection. It has been stripped of its dependence on natural reasoning and rebuilt with divine intelligence. This mind is not fueled by the opinions of men, the traditions of religion, or the limitations of human education. It is a mind **filled with new knowledge**—knowledge that flows from the Throne Room of Heaven.

This knowledge is not academic. It is not
the result of research or religious study. It is
revelatory, born of the Spirit, and hidden in
God. It carries the very **blueprints of creation**,
the thoughts of the Creator released into the
heart of the created. It is not carnal or sensual,
nor is it based on facts. **It is divine truth.**
Eternal, incorruptible, and unshakable.

The Custodian of Divine Thought

God is the custodian of this knowledge. He
is the keeper of divine intelligence, and He
releases it according to His will. This is not
information that can be earned—it must be
revealed.

*"Which were born, not of blood, nor of the
will of the flesh, nor of the will of man, but of
God."*
—John 1:13

The New Man is born of God and,
therefore, qualifies to receive what only God
can give. This access is not granted by
credentials, denominations, or doctrinal
alignment. No college degree can unlock it. No
seminary can teach it. **No religious title can**

guarantee it. This is a knowledge reserved for **sons**, and the only door is **Jesus Christ**.

He is the **Way** because there is no alternate route.

He is the **Truth** because all other knowledge must bow.

He is the **Life** because only in Him can this mind function.

The Death of the Old Mind

Before this new mind can live, the old one must die. This is not a gentle transition. The carnal mind is **hostile** to God (Romans 8:7). It cannot comprehend His ways, trust His word, or sustain His presence. It is limited, fearful, self-seeking, and bound by earthly logic. It cannot produce the God-life in the earth.

Therefore, it must die.

Transformation is not behavior modification—it is resurrection. **The mind of the New Man is one that has been crucified.** It is a mind that confessed its inability to serve Heaven while being shaped by earth. It surrendered. It was buried. And now it lives again—reborn, renewed, reformed by the Spirit of God.

A Mind That Proves the Will of God

Romans 12:2 gives us the key:
"Be ye transformed by the renewing of your mind, that ye may prove what is that good, and acceptable, and perfect, will of God."

The renewed mind is **proof**. It becomes the evidence of heaven's will. The way you think, decide, lead, and speak should be a demonstration of what pleases the Father. The renewed mind discerns what the natural man dismisses. It recognizes divine order. It sees kingdom patterns. It responds to heaven's frequency.

It's not a mind influenced by headlines or social media feeds—it's a mind **anchored in eternity**.

Revelation Is the New Intelligence

The intelligence of the New Man is a revelation. Not emotion. Not logic. Not tradition. But revealed truth from God's Spirit to your spirit.

You don't need worldly IQ—you need **divine perception**. The Spirit searches all things, even the deep things of God, and reveals them to those who have His mind (1 Corinthians 2:10–16). This is why the New Man lives differently. He makes decisions that seem foolish to the carnal but make perfect sense in the Spirit.

He doesn't move by fear. He moves by insight.

He doesn't speak to impress. He speaks to **create**.

He doesn't follow the crowd. He follows the **cloud**.

You Have the Mind of Christ

Paul declares, *"But we have the mind of Christ"* (1 Corinthians 2:16). That's not a suggestion—it's a statement of reality. The New Man has access to divine thought. You are no longer stuck trying to figure out your purpose with a broken compass. The compass has been replaced with the **counsel of heaven**.

To live from this mind is to live from above. To think from this place is to command from a higher dimension. And to embrace this mind is to say, "I no longer rely on what I knew—I now move by what God is revealing."

This is the mind of the New Man. It is alive. It is divine. And it is yours.

Prayer for the Mind of the New Man

Father, thank You for giving me the mind of Christ. Thank You that I am no longer conformed to the patterns of this world but transformed by the renewing of my mind.

Let every thought in me align with truth. Let every stronghold of the old man be torn down. Let every lie be cast out and replaced with revelation. I receive the divine knowledge that flows from Your throne. I receive the mind that is led by Your Spirit.

Help me to see from above. Help me to hear with clarity. Help me to walk in purpose. Let boldness rise in me—boldness to speak, to lead, to believe, and to manifest the life You have placed within me.

This is not just a new season. It is a new mind. And I receive it by faith.

In Jesus' name, Amen.

CHAPTER 4:
THE LIFE OF THE NEW CREATION

Scripture Foundation: Galatians 2:20; Proverbs 22:9; Colossians 3:10; John 3:16; Philippians 4:19

"I am crucified with Christ: nevertheless I live; yet not I, but Christ liveth in me: and the life which I now live in the flesh I live by the faith of the Son of God, who loved me, and gave himself for me."
—Galatians 2:20

The New Creation doesn't live from opinion, culture, or preference—it lives from the **same source that gave it birth: Christ Himself**. This is not an improved life; it is a **resurrected life** made possible by divine exchange. It is not yours to manage—it is **His to live through you**.

When Paul said, *"I am crucified with Christ,"* he wasn't speaking metaphorically. He meant the old self, the old appetites, the self-centered motives—all of it—**died**. And what now lives is a **Christ-empowered life** sourced from the very heart of Heaven.

This life flows in perfect alignment with God's nature. And at the core of that nature is **giving**.

The Nature of Giving

"For God so loved the world, that He gave…"

Giving is not just something God does—it is **who He is**. The New Creation, made in His image, reflects that same nature. This means that **giving is not a task—it's a lifestyle**. The life of the New Man flows from generosity, not just of money, but of time, wisdom, love, honor, and resources.

"He that hath a bountiful eye shall be blessed; for he giveth of his bread to the poor." —Proverbs 22:9

The New Creation **sees differently**. It doesn't look at what's lacking—it looks at what's available. It doesn't hold tightly out of fear—it releases freely out of faith. This life trusts in the unlimited flow of Heaven's supply.

30

Heaven Can't Flow Through Closed Hands

The Spirit of God is generous. He pours out, He multiplies, He overflows. But He won't pour through hands that are clenched with fear or self-preservation. **Self must die** for Heaven to flow.

The person who still lives for themselves cannot be trusted with divine resources. Why? Because they'll build their own empire instead of God's. But the New Man—the one who has died to self and now lives by the faith of the Son—can be trusted with the **wealth of Heaven**.

This is why the New Creation doesn't beg. It doesn't hoard. It doesn't manipulate. It receives, releases, and repeats. It knows that **"My God shall supply all your need according to His riches in glory by Christ Jesus"** (Philippians 4:19). The supply doesn't run out because the Source doesn't run dry.

Heaven's Distribution Center

You are not just a recipient—you are a **conduit**. The New Creation is **Heaven's distribution center** in the Earth. When God wants to bless a family, a community, a church, or a nation, He looks for a vessel that carries His heart and lives by His supply.

That vessel is the New Man.

He's not distracted by scarcity.
He's not bound by fear.
He knows the assignment: **Receive from Heaven, release to the earth.**

And this distribution doesn't just include finances. It includes wisdom, revelation, leadership, healing, strategy, prophetic insight, and divine timing. Wherever the New Creation goes, **needs are met**—because Heaven moves through them.

The Spirit of Excellence and Royalty

The mindset of the New Creation is not casual—it is **royal**. You are a son of the King. You are seated with Christ. And because of that, **everything you do should reflect Heaven's standards**.

"Put on the new man, which is renewed in knowledge after the image of him that created him."
—Colossians 3:10

This new man carries the image of the King and should function like royalty. Royalty doesn't cut corners. Royalty doesn't move in dishonor. Royalty doesn't slack.

The spirit of excellence is the **standard** of the Kingdom. And excellence is not perfection—it is intentionality. It is doing all things as unto the Lord. And when excellence flows from you, **promotion follows**. You don't chase platforms—they come to you. You don't beg for influence—it's given because you can be trusted.

No Slackness, Only Faith

The life of the New Creation is not lazy. It is not passive. It is not waiting on "one day." It is **faith-filled and purpose-driven**. There is no slackness in the one who lives by the **faith of the Son of God**.

This is not just believing in Jesus. This is believing **with** Jesus—operating from the same faith that raised the dead, healed the sick, multiplied provision, and obeyed the Father without fear.

The life you live now is divine. It is generous. It is excellent. It is powerful. It is trustworthy.

This is the life of the New Creation.

Prayer for the Life of the New Creation

Father, I thank You for the new life You have given me in Christ. Thank You that I am no longer bound to my old ways, my old mind, or my old nature. I have been crucified with Christ, and now I live by His faith and power.

Let my life reflect Your giving heart. Let generosity be my posture. Let excellence be my standard. Use me as a channel of blessing—a distribution center for the needs of others. I open my hands. I open my heart. I receive from Heaven, and I release it in love.

Teach me to walk in royalty. To think with the mind of a son. To operate with honor. To serve with power. Let there be no slackness in me but only purpose and pursuit.

I embrace this new life. I steward it well. And I live it by faith.

In Jesus' name, Amen.

CHAPTER 5:

THE INFLUENCE AND DESIGN OF THE NEW CREATION

Scripture Foundation: Romans 8:19; Psalm 139:14; John 4:24; Matthew 5:13

"For the earnest expectation of the creature waiteth for the manifestation of the sons of God."
—Romans 8:19

The earth is not confused—it is **expectant**. It's not falling apart because God has lost control. It's groaning in anticipation. For what? For **you.** For me. For the **manifestation of the sons of God**.

This world isn't waiting on religion. It's not waiting on another conference, another building, or another brand of church. It's waiting on the **New Creation** to step fully into its identity and release what's already inside. The earth is yearning for the emergence of people who understand the **covenant they're**

under, the **material they're made of**, and the **assignment they've been given**.

Spirit: The Material of Dominion

"God is a Spirit: and they that worship him must worship him in spirit and in truth."
—John 4:24

The New Creation is not made of flesh and blood, doctrine and denomination, or personality and performance. We are made of **spirit**. That's the material God used to form us. And the **material of a thing determines the design of the thing** (Psalm 139:14).

When God said, "Let us make man in our image, after our likeness," He was declaring more than shape—He was declaring **substance**. If God is Spirit, then His offspring must also be Spirit. We are **Spirit-born**, Spirit-filled, and Spirit-assigned.

That's why you can't live your calling in the flesh. The power you carry isn't designed to be sustained by ego, talent, or intellect. **Only your spirit can hold what Heaven placed in you.**

And because you are spirit, you can:

- **Receive spiritual revelation**
- **Operate in supernatural authority**
- **Release the atmosphere of Heaven into the earth**

You are made of the **same creative material as your Creator.** That means the capacity to **speak, shape, build, shift, and transform** is not something you beg for—it's embedded in your design.

The New Creation Carries the Creator's DNA

We don't just belong to God—we come from Him.

Paul said, *"We are His offspring."* That's not a metaphor—it's a spiritual fact. **You have His spiritual DNA.** And that DNA carries:

- His creativity
- His integrity
- His compassion
- His excellence
- His power
- His dominion

You're not trying to be like God—you were *made* like God. Sin distorted the image, but the New Covenant restored the blueprint. And now the New Creation walks the earth again—**fully authorized**, fully equipped, and fully awakened.

Salt: The Power of Influence

"You are the salt of the earth…"
—Matthew 5:13

The New Creation is not passive—it's **potent**. Salt never enters an environment quietly. It doesn't take sides—it **takes over**. Salt influences whatever it touches. It preserves. It enhances. It heals. It stops decay.

You are not here to **blend in**. You are here to **transform**. And transformation only happens when we walk in the fullness of who we are. We are not here to fit into culture—we are here to **redefine it**.

Kingdom Colonization: Heaven's Strategy

No ambassador is sent to another country to adopt that country's ways. A true ambassador brings the language, economy, values, and vision of their **home country** into the one they've been sent to.

That is **Kingdom colonization**.

You were not saved just to go to Heaven—you were born again to **bring Heaven here**. You carry Heaven's mindset, Heaven's culture, Heaven's honor, and Heaven's power. You are a walking embassy of the Kingdom. Your presence shifts the atmosphere, not because of who you are in the flesh, but because of who you are **in Christ**.

You are not here to be impressed by Babylon—you are here to **bring Zion**.

The Manifestation Is Now

Romans 8:19 isn't about one day. It's about **right now**. Creation is waiting for sons who know who they are. Daughters who walk in dominion. Believers who release the kingdom. Not performers. Not pretenders. **Sons.**

You are not waiting on revival. **You are revival.** You are Heaven's strategy in the earth. And the moment you believe that—you become unstoppable.

This is your moment.

The world is watching.

Creation is groaning.

Heaven is backing you.

Manifest.

Prayer for Manifesting as a New Creation

Father, I thank You that I am not who I used to be. I am born of You—not of flesh, not of will, but of Spirit. You have made me in Your image, after Your likeness, and You have placed Your DNA in me.

Let me manifest the reality of this divine nature. Let the world see the reflection of Heaven in how I live, speak, and love. I reject every label of my past. I silence every lie of unworthiness. I declare that I am who You say I am.

Make me bold. Make me excellent. Make me a living demonstration of what it means to walk in sonship. I receive my assignment. I embrace my authority. I release the influence of Heaven everywhere I go.

In Jesus' name, Amen.

CHAPTER 6

THE SUPERNATURAL BIRTH OF THE NEW CREATION

Scripture Foundation: John 3:6; Ephesians 2:4–6; Ephesians 3:14–19; Hebrews 12:24; Philippians 2:9–11

"That which is born of the flesh is flesh, and that which is born of the Spirit is spirit."
—John 3:6

The New Creation was not born of man—it was born of God. Its birth was **supernatural**, its origin is **eternal**, and its nature is **divine**. This is not a metaphor. This is not theology. This is **truth**—truth that carries **power** because it reveals who we truly are and **where we truly belong**.

The supernatural birth of the New Creation has **sealed its eternal home**. No more striving to earn a place at the table. No more trying to climb into favor with God. **You are born from above**, and your spirit now **lives and abides forever**.

This new life is not limited by time, space, bloodline, or background. It is a life **without limits** because it is a life **filled with the Spirit without measure**. There is no restriction in your inheritance. No cap on your access. **The same Spirit that raised Christ from the dead now lives in you.**

The Power of the Family Name

In this new birth, you also receive a new name—a family name. And this name carries **supreme authority**.

"Wherefore God also hath highly exalted him, and given him a name which is above every name... that at the name of Jesus every knee should bow..."
—Philippians 2:9–10

There is **no name greater** in heaven or earth. And you are not just called by this name—you are **born into it**. The New Creation carries the **family seal**. The power in the name of Jesus is not only for spiritual warfare—it is for identity. You live in that name. You pray in that name. You operate in that name.

And when you speak from that name, **creation responds**.

The Blood That Bonds Us

The glue that holds this eternal family together is not tradition, denomination, or church attendance. It is the **blood of Christ**.

"The blood of sprinkling, that speaketh better things than that of Abel."
—Hebrews 12:24

The blood still speaks—and its voice is louder than your past. The blood declares:

- You are **washed** clean

- You are **justified** by faith

- You are **made righteous**

- You are **seated with Christ**

This is not wishful thinking—it is a **heavenly reality**. You are not climbing into righteousness—you've already been seated in it. You are not becoming holy—you've been made holy. The New Creation is not on its way to identity—it is **sealed** in it.

A Family Beyond the Flesh

"We know no man after the flesh..."
—2 Corinthians 5:16

In this family, **your genealogy is canceled out**. Your bloodline has been overwritten. The curses of your past have no legal access here. You have been born into a **new family**, and this family is **spiritual**, eternal, and governed by love.

You are **bonded together with other believers**, not by agreement, but by spirit. There are no fall-outs in this family because we don't war after the flesh. Our agenda is not competition—it's **the King's agenda**. Our culture is not built on race, preference, or tradition—it is built on the **Word of God**, which is the **constitution of our Kingdom**.

You were born again by the Word (1 Peter 1:23), and you are sustained by it. Everything about you now flows from the same source that gave you life: the **unshakable, eternal Word of God**.

Love: The Realm of Revelation

You are not just born again—you are **rooted and grounded in love** (Ephesians 3:17). And that love gives you supernatural comprehension.

"That you may be able to comprehend with all saints what is the breadth, and length, and depth, and height..."
—Ephesians 3:18

Love unlocks understanding. It's not just an emotion—it is the **realm where revelation lives**. It is in love that you discover how deep the Father's plans go. How high your seat truly is. How wide your inheritance stretches. And how full your life can really become.

Will You Receive the Truth?

The only question left is: **Will you receive this?**

Not just read it.

Not just nod to it.

But receive it—**deep in your spirit**.

The world has labeled you. Religion has tried to define you. Your past has tried to hold you. But **God has spoken**—you are **a new**

creation, born of God, seated in Christ, and part of an unbreakable eternal family.

This is who you are.

This is what you carry.

This is the time to rise.

Welcome home.

Prayer for the Supernatural Family of God

Heavenly Father, I come to You today asking for insight and understanding into the supernatural family I've been born into. Reveal to me the depth, nature, and power of the family name—**the name of Jesus**. Help me to walk in it, live from it, speak out of it, and take my rightful place without fear, doubt, or a sense of inferiority.

I thank You that the blood still speaks. The blood declares that I am washed, justified by faith, made righteous, and seated with Christ on the throne. Stretch me, Lord. Take my life beyond limits—beyond borders I've never imagined.

Work the impossible through me to make it possible for others. Give me revelation-filled words that ignite faith and awaken new identity in believers. Cause my life to reflect Your divine will and Your heavenly ways.

I thank You for this new life You've given me—and now I trust You to help me live it to the fullest.

In Jesus' name, Amen.

CHAPTER 7:

IN HIM IS THE NEW LIFE

Scripture Foundation: John 10:10; John 1:1–4; Genesis 1:26–28; Psalm 119:105; Colossians 3:1–3

"I am come that they might have life, and that they might have it more abundantly."
—John 10:10

There is no life in the graveyard. Only echoes. Only memories of what *could have been*—books unwritten, dreams unfulfilled, missions left incomplete. That is **not your story**.

You are not buried—you are **resurrected**.

The dead things that once held you couldn't keep you. The tomb that tried to close in around you was rolled open by **resurrection power**. You are **risen with Christ**, the Resurrected King. And the identity of the New Creation is no longer a concept—it is **alive in you**.

The grave has no claim.

The past has no power.

The stone is rolled away.

You Hold the Keys Now

What once locked you out has now been handed into your hands. **The keys of the Kingdom**—access, authority, and dominion—have been returned to the sons. The chains are broken, not because of effort but because of inheritance. The same Spirit that raised Jesus from the dead has raised **you**.

You no longer walk in circles of defeat. You walk in the pathway of the King.

"He has come to give life and life more abundantly." That life isn't coming. **It's already here.** You're not waiting to live—you've already been made alive. But the key now is this: **You must focus.**

The Power of Focused Hearing

The world is loud. The enemy is deceptive. But you were never called to follow the noise—you were called to follow **His voice**.

"My sheep hear My voice, and a stranger's voice they will not follow."

There is a frequency from the Throne Room that belongs to the sons. It cuts through chaos. It overrides confusion. It's the same frequency that called Lazarus out of the grave—and now it calls **you** into purpose. Our King calls **audibles**—in-the-moment instructions designed to confuse the enemy and execute the will of Heaven.

That's why **intentional focus** matters. The Word of God is not just a book—it's a **GPS**. It speaks. It guides. It adjusts in real-time to ensure your victory. You don't need to be afraid of the unknown. You only need to follow His voice.

Dead Things Cannot Produce Living Purpose

The believer must stop trying to extract life from dead places.

- Dead relationships
- Dead religion
- Dead patterns

- Dead thoughts

These things **move not**. They **produce not**. And they cannot sustain resurrection life.

Your new life is **only found in Him**. He is the Alpha and the Omega—the One who knows the end from the beginning. You don't need to chase signs—you just need to stay in step with the Word. And the Word is not distant—it's **in you**.

You Are Authorized by the Creator

When God gave dominion to man in Genesis 1:26–28, **creation heard it**. Every element, every system, every force on the earth **recognized your authority**. The earth responds to you not because of your humanity but because of your **divine image**. You were created to command. You were authorized to subdue. You were empowered to multiply.

And how do you do it?

With the Word.

"Thy Word is a lamp unto my feet and a light unto my path."

"The Word was with God, and the Word was God… and that same Word is in you."

Faith-Filled Speech Brings Resurrection Results

The Word is not just a sound—it is a **seed**. And when it's planted in a heart full of faith, it produces results that confuse the enemy and glorify God.

You are not speaking in vain.

You are not prophesying to the air.

You are commanding systems, shifting atmospheres, and releasing the will of God **with your voice**.

The Word in your mouth is the same Word that formed the universe. And when it is spoken in faith—it **must produce**.

So speak.

Live.

Move.

Declare.

The grave has been defeated.

The stone has been rolled away.

The King has risen—and so have you.

In Him is the New Life—and that life is yours.

Prayer for Resurrection Life and Sonship

Father, I pray that this divine call to Sonship has been heard and answered. Let the impartation of the words in this book now become active and alive in every heart that has read and received them by faith. As Your son, I now activate this truth.

Let there be an expectancy in this generation—an awakening to produce miracles, signs, and wonders like never before. We stand ready, bold, and yielded to witness and declare Your glory in the earth.

Let the heavens rejoice, for an army has arisen. The dead have come to life. The grave has no power. The Word has spoken, and we respond with faith.

Miracles, signs, and wonders are our portion. We rightfully receive, in Jesus' name. Amen.

Conclusion

To all who have journeyed through the pages of this book, thank you.

Your hunger for truth and your willingness to embrace the revelation of who you are in Christ means more than words can say. This book was written not just to inspire but to activate. Not just to teach but to transform. And if you have received, believed, and embraced even one truth within these pages—you are already walking in greater glory.

You are a New Creature. You are seated in heavenly places. You are filled with the Spirit of God and called to manifest His Kingdom on earth. Don't stop here. Keep walking in the light of this revelation. Speak it. Live it. Share it.

Thank you for purchasing and reading this volume. I pray it has been fuel to your spirit and fire to your faith.

And this is only the beginning.

Stay connected and stay expectant— **Volume II** is on the horizon. It will go deeper, stretch further, and continue building the foundation that has been laid.

Until then, keep manifesting. Keep advancing. Keep becoming.

The world is waiting on the real you.

With gratitude and expectation,

Apostle, Dr. Craig A. Comanche

www.ingramcontent.com/pod-product-compliance
Lightning Source LLC
Chambersburg PA
CBHW070943120626
46546CB00004B/1546